Hide not your Talents, they for Use were made.

What's a Sun-Dial in the shade!

—POOR RICHARD'S ALMANACK, 1750

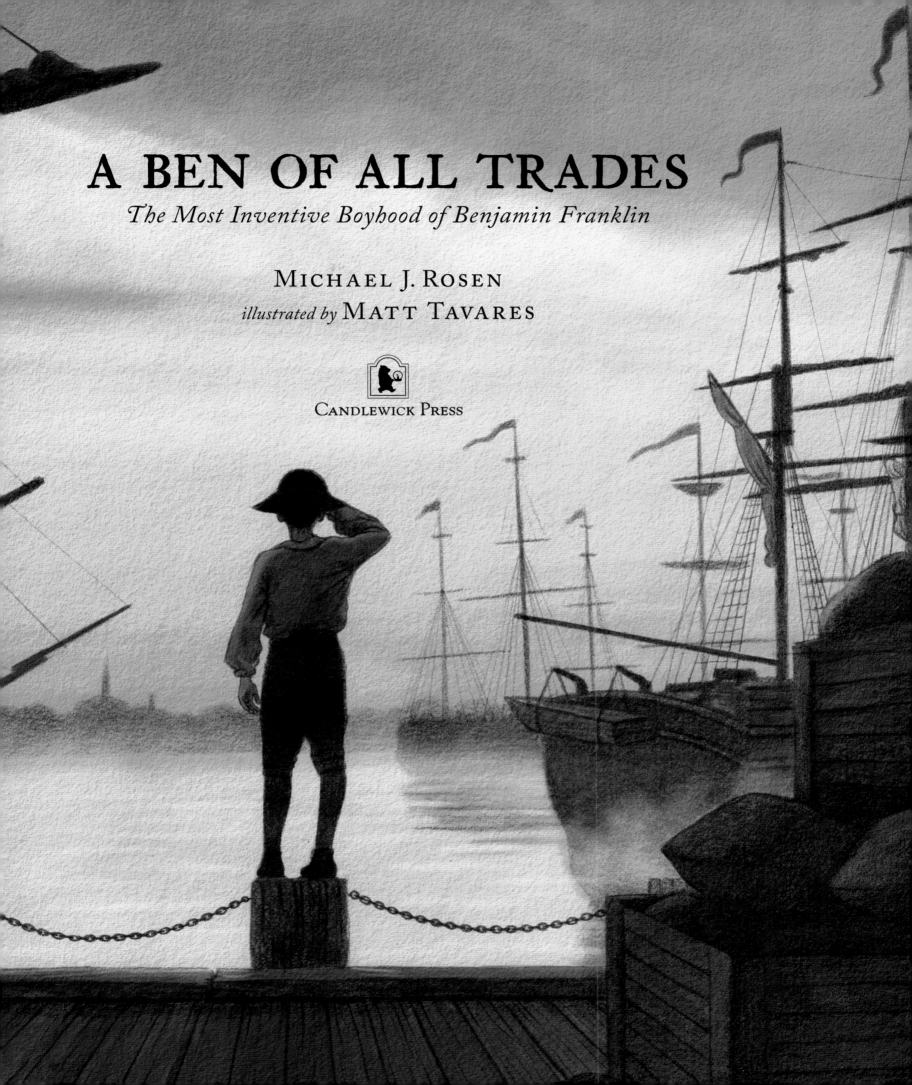

A BEN OF ALL TRADES

The Most Inventive Boyhood of Benjamin Franklin

MICHAEL J. ROSEN

illustrated by MATT TAVARES

CANDLEWICK PRESS

WHAT DID Benjamin Franklin love about books? Each one was nothing like another.

What did Benjamin *not* love about making candles? Each one was, in every way, like others.

He measured wicks, melted tallow, and thickened each candle—dipping . . . dipping . . . dipping . . . daydreaming. His father desperately needed to find his son a trade that suited his talents. But practicing swimming strokes? Endlessly reading? All Benjamin desired was to be a sailor. All he appeared to be was an aimless woolgatherer. Lately, the boy was obsessed with *The Art of Swimming,* a book from his father's library. In the light of his own hand's identical candles, he had studied every stroke.

Neck deep and naked in Mill Pond, Benjamin gripped two wooden paddles he'd carved.

"Ten, nine, eight . . ." his sister Lydia counted down. "Go!"

Gulping air, Benjamin bounded forward, whirling his arms. His paddles spanked and tugged the water beneath him. *Whap, whoosh . . . whap, whoosh . . .* His kicking churned a bubbly wake. *Hhhhhuueep!*—lifting his head, he sucked in air again. *Whap, whoosh . . . whap, whoosh . . .*

Finally at the dock, he spun around.

"Forty seconds!" Lydia exclaimed. "*Twice* as fast!"

At supper, a very excited Benjamin presented his fins.

"Thumbs go in these holes." He slipped on the paddles. "They afford your hands the mightiest power!"

"Quite inventive. Truly," his father, Josiah, pronounced. "But no. My answer's still no."

"Father! I'd be a superb sailor!"

"The sea has shown no benevolence to our family," Josiah said. "Besides, candles are something people always need."

"I fear my mind is unsuited for the craft, sir."

Benjamin begged Lydia and his friend John Collins to join him at the pond. "What's that?" John called to Benjamin as he waved his friend's shirt overhead.

"Swimming Neither on Back nor Belly."

"Now, what's *that*?"

"Swimming with Left Foot in Right Hand."

"But . . . why?" shouted Lydia.

"Should a leg suffer a cramp, I'm prepared!"

"This week," Josiah announced at breakfast, "you shall apprentice with a joiner. Mind you, Benjamin, a trade needn't be to your liking. But perhaps joinery will engage your restlessness."

The hours at the joiners were like treading water for Benjamin. They exhausted him and yet he never moved from the same position at the workbench. Even by the third day, he doubted he could last to the week's end.

When Josiah arrived to retrieve his son, he found Benjamin sanding a timber peg, both knees straddling a bucket brimming with identical pegs.

Following the Charles River toward home, Josiah still sought a clear answer from his son: "What say you of joinery, Benjamin?"

"I fear it is not for me. Sanding and drilling and fitting the same joints over and over is hardly agreeable. But a seaman . . . if only you'd let me—"

"You *know* my answer . . . *and yet you ask*? I will find you a trade lest you play the truant and run to the sea."

When the path bent toward the shoreline, Benjamin grinned. "Father, might I show you what I've practiced?" He stripped, waded into the river, tied his ankles together with his belt, and plunged beneath the surface.

Half a minute later, his head popped up and his arms swept in half circles, all but his shoulders held above the water.

"Your legs? You've yoked them?" Josiah asked.

"Yes! It's called To Swim with Legs Tied."

"Ludicrous."

"*Logical!* In case weeds ever entangle my legs."

"Come out of that filthy water at once."

The following week, Benjamin apprenticed with a boot closer. But sewing together the uppers of shoe after shoe after shoe—Benjamin had no penchant for that.

The same was true of the turner's trade the following week: chiseling wood into smooth dowels, one dowel exactly like the one before. . . .

When Josiah came to collect his son, he could see Benjamin's forlorn face. "*Nothing* suits, son? Nothing? You do realize daydreaming won't provide a living."

"I don't *aim* to disappoint, sir."

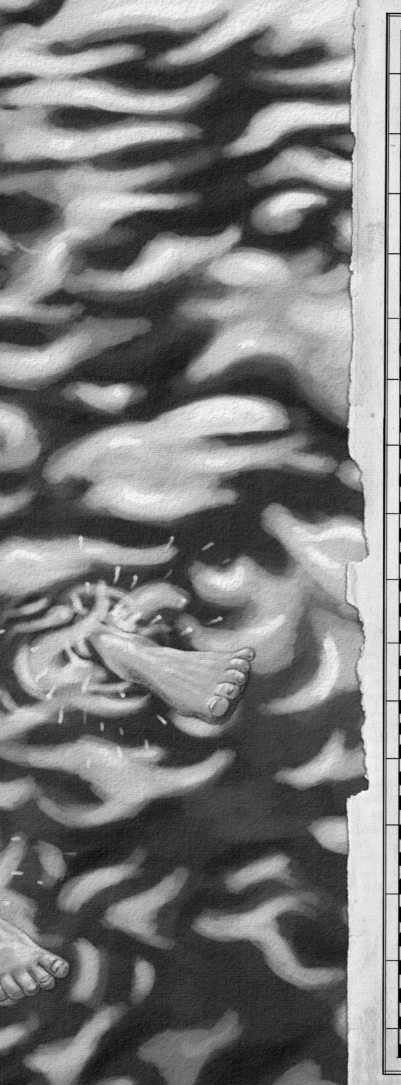

The two walked without speaking until they approached the river. "Father, I've learned the Leap of the Goat. It's the feat that shows *true mastery* of the swimming arts."

"If you *must* demonstrate, then you must. . . ."

Benjamin raced toward the water. Floating on his back, chest inflated, he thrashed his arms against the sun-bright ripples until his feet fluttered inches above the river.

Josiah applauded.

Benjamin dressed.

The two walked home in silence.

The next days, strong winds lashed Boston and Benjamin spent his free hours fashioning a kite. One especially gusty afternoon, he enlisted Lydia and John to accompany him to Mill Pond. Holding a stick with spooled string, Benjamin set off running.

"Need help? You can barely hold it!" shouted John. "*It's* pulling *you*!"

The paper diamond volleyed back and forth, west to east, as if it were uncertain as to which direction was up.

Suddenly another of Benjamin's ideas snatched the moment. He tethered the kite string around a stake, stripped, and shouted, "I'm going in!"

Shoulders deep and kite in hand, Benjamin called, "Won't you take my clothes, John, to the opposite bank?"

Unfurling the spool, the wind harnessed in the kite jolted
Benjamin onto his back and towed him, zigzagging, across the pond
within a minute—far faster than even his strongest stroke.
"Such power . . . and from nothing but air!" Lydia exclaimed.

Single file on the deer-hoof-stamped trail that encircled the pond, Lydia, John, and Benjamin wended the paths toward home.

His hair still dripping, his arms hugging the sodden kite, Benjamin met Josiah outside their house. "What *is* to come of this, Benjamin? You devote your hours to swimming—now with a kite, no less!—and yet you dismiss every trade you're offered."

"I have no affinity for those, Father, it's true—yet that time was hardly ill spent. I've kept all that I acquired. The kite's frame I chiseled smooth because I learned *that* from the turner. The joint's holes and pegs? The joiner taught me. The paper itself, I painted with *our* tallow, Father, so the kite would float."

"I see," Josiah said.

"And from the boot closer, I knew to lace the kite to its frame."

Dry and in fresh clothes, Benjamin found Josiah
in the library preparing his decision.

"So. Neither joiner nor boot closer, neither turner
nor chandler . . . you're a Benjamin of *all trades*—
is that your desire?"

"No . . . I don't know. My straightest desire is to
be aboard—"

"Son of mine, I will *not* see another Franklin lost
to the sea.

"I fear there's no alternative but for you to sign the
indentures with your brother James. You'll be a
journeyman at his print shop. And there, perhaps you
will read and study and write to the contentment of
your heart."

"I will endeavor to do so," said Benjamin. "But I
do wish his shop were seaworthy!"

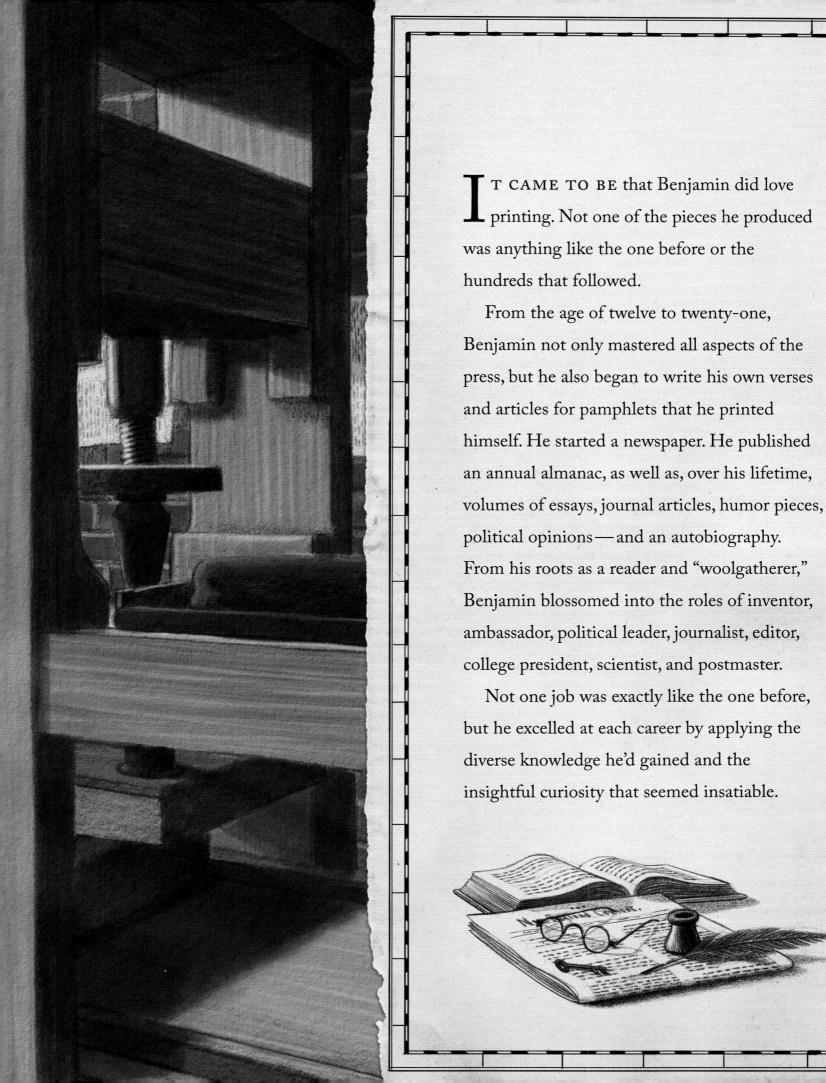

IT CAME TO BE that Benjamin did love printing. Not one of the pieces he produced was anything like the one before or the hundreds that followed.

From the age of twelve to twenty-one, Benjamin not only mastered all aspects of the press, but he also began to write his own verses and articles for pamphlets that he printed himself. He started a newspaper. He published an annual almanac, as well as, over his lifetime, volumes of essays, journal articles, humor pieces, political opinions — and an autobiography. From his roots as a reader and "woolgatherer," Benjamin blossomed into the roles of inventor, ambassador, political leader, journalist, editor, college president, scientist, and postmaster.

Not one job was exactly like the one before, but he excelled at each career by applying the diverse knowledge he'd gained and the insightful curiosity that seemed insatiable.

About Young Franklin

BENJAMIN FRANKLIN was born in 1706. For seventy more years—until the War of Independence—America remained a colony of the British empire. An Englishman at birth, he died an American in 1790.

The eighth of ten children born to Josiah Franklin and Abiah Folger, Benjamin, a gifted reader, seemed a good candidate for the clergy. However, after Ben had studied for two years, his family felt they could no longer afford such education. Thus, Benjamin needed a trade. In colonial times, a boy—and sometimes, rarely, a girl—apprenticed to a tradesman for a specified number of years. In exchange for the experience and the instruction, the apprentice, called a journeyman, would be housed and fed. Upon the contract's fulfillment, the apprentice became a "freeman," permitted to practice the craft independently.

Benjamin pleaded to become a sailor. (He loved swimming, in an era before swimming pools or even bathing suits.) His father's opposition to this choice was fierce, however, as he had already lost his namesake, Josiah Franklin Jr. (1685–1715), to nine years on the sea, with no news of his fate. Thus Benjamin was forced to consider other trades, including his father's own soap- and candle-making business. But all his visits with a variety of tradesmen ended unsatisfyingly.

Ultimately, his father committed Benjamin to apprentice at his brother James's printing shop. These experiences launched Benjamin's gifts as a true polymath: a person whose knowledge and talents span a wide range of subjects and disciplines. Not only did he become one of this country's Founding Fathers, but he also helped draft the Constitution and the Declaration of Independence, negotiated the treaty that ended the Revolutionary War, and served as America's first ambassador to France. More than two centuries later, many consider Benjamin Franklin the most accomplished American of his era.

About Creating This Book

THE STORY told here is inspired by Franklin's *Memoirs*, written at age sixty-five. The book, which came to be known as *The Autobiography of Benjamin Franklin* and was published after his lifetime, is considered the first book of literature by an American to reach a large, worldwide audience. His earlier collections of sayings, weather predictions, wit, and lore, *Poor Richard's Almanack* (an annual published from 1732 to 1758), were so popular that they shaped the character of this country. His proverbs, predictions, verses, humor, and opinions commended the virtues of thriftiness, hard work, humility, justice, moderation, and using time well.

Writing from a distance of some fifty years, Franklin's memories were the sole resource he had for composing the cultured and studied sentences for his autobiography. It delivers little in the way of details or description. Dialogue is not present. And more to the point of this story: he was not composing a picture book. He had no thought to craft a tale for young readers.

So that is where I come in, figuring how to bring this story to life for *you*. Writers and illustrators both make choices about what to include and what to leave out. Does a painting include every leaf on a tree? Does a page of prose give the name of every item in a tool shed or basement? Hardly. A great part of all creativity is selection. Making these additions, I focused on keeping the culture, temperament, language, and circumstances of Franklin's life and era.

I worked to open out Franklin's brief recollections in order to compose a realistic story you would enjoy. All conversations here are my invention, using word choices and speech patterns of the era found in Franklin biographies and sources about colonial times.

Benjamin's autobiography doesn't state that his sister clocked his speed as he swam with paddles. A sentence *does* report that his fins increased his speed, even as they tired his wrists. A logical idea was that Lydia, to whom he was closest, might have timed him.

There's no reference to his father watching him demonstrate the various swimming strokes from *The Art of Swimming*. But the book *was* present in Josiah's library, just as his father was most present in his son's upbringing.

Franklin's autobiography says "another boy" carried his clothes to the opposite shore when the kite dragged him across the pond. But Franklin's fondness for Lydia and John are well documented, and I believed that including them in this scene gave a fuller picture of Benjamin's character.

As for the scene in which he explains to his father how he has applied the skills the various tradesmen have taught him, I've drawn that from elsewhere in the autobiography, where he writes, near the end of his exceptionally eclectic life, "It has proved of considerable benefit, to have acquired thereby sufficient knowledge to be able to make little things for myself, when I had no mechanic at hand, and to construct small machines for my experiments." So I drew upon this idea, which so perfectly reflects Franklin's passion for experience and information, as a way for Ben to justify his crafting of the kite. Now, *that* sort of reasoning is something Franklin himself enjoyed: imagining possibilities with his own extensive knowledge, intuitive analysis, and wild creativity.

From the Illustrator

I GREW UP just outside of Boston. So when I first read this story, I was excited about the chance to illustrate my hometown in its early days. I imagined scenes from Benjamin Franklin's childhood against a backdrop of landmarks I knew so well—the Old South Meeting House, Faneuil Hall, the Old North Church.

But I soon learned that the Boston of Benjamin Franklin's childhood was not the Boston that I envisioned. When young Benjamin was splashing around in the Charles River and the Mill Pond, none of these famous landmarks had even been built yet.

Back then, Boston was a bustling peninsula, with one road connecting it to the mainland, and a population of seven thousand. But there were over a thousand ships registered at its harbor. From his home at the corner of Union and Hanover Streets, Ben had to walk only a block or two in any direction to reach the water. It's no wonder young Benjamin longed for a life at sea. He was surrounded by it!

I tried to incorporate elements of his life into this book. I used pages from antique books as backgrounds for the text panels, to represent the importance of books, both in Ben's early days and throughout his life. The borders that surround the text panels are inspired by colonial-era nautical maps, to represent young Benjamin's longing for the sea and his quest to navigate his way in the world.

While I was doing research for this book, one thing that made me smile was learning that during his lifetime, Benjamin Franklin crossed the Atlantic Ocean eight times. He set sail for the first time at the age of eighteen and made his final transatlantic voyage when he was seventy-nine. These were perilous, harrowing journeys that could take as long as two or three months. So even though he never disobeyed his father by running off to sea, his childhood dream did eventually come true.

I would like to thank the following people who helped bring this book to life: Sarah, Matt, and Nate Hall; Ava, Molly, and Sarah Tavares; Eric Fan, Ryan Higgins, Scott Magoon, Rosemary Stimola, Katie Cunningham, and Maryellen Hanley; and special thanks to Drew Hall, for kindly posing as a young Benjamin Franklin, and for continuing to swim even as my homemade cardboard paddles disintegrated.

Bibliography

BOOKS

Franklin, Benjamin. *Benjamin Franklin's Autobiography: An Authoritative Text, Backgrounds, Criticism.* Edited by J. A. Leo Lamay and P. M. Zall. Norton Critical Edition. New York: Norton, 1986.

———. *Poor Richard's Almanack, and Other Writings.* Mineola, NY: Dover Publications, 2013.

Hawke, David Freeman. *Everyday Life in Early America.* New York: Harper & Row, 1988.

Isaacson, Walter. *Benjamin Franklin: An American Life.* New York: Simon & Schuster, 2004.

WEBSITE

Ben Franklin: An Extraordinary Life, An Electric Mind. Public Broadcasting Service. http://www.pbs.org/benfranklin/.

*For all who've joined in
the swim with me*

M. J. R.

*For the Bloodwells—
Daisy, Charlie, Michelle, and Ben*

M. T.